SURVIVING THE UNSURVIVABLE

A True Account of Love and Loss

By: Ms Kathy Johnson

Copyright @2021 by Kathy Johnson

All rights reserved. No part of this book may be reproduced in any form or by any electronic or mechanical means, including information storage and retrieval systems, without permission in writing from the publisher, except by reviewers, who may quote brief passages in a review.

This publication contains the opinions and ideas of its author. It is intended to provide helpful and informative material on the subjects addressed in the publication. The author and publisher specifically disclaim all responsibility for any liability, loss or risk, personal or otherwise, which is incurred as a consequence, directly or indirectly, of the use and application of any of the contents of this book.

WORKBOOK PRESS LLC
187 E Warm Springs Rd,
Suite B285, Las Vegas, NV 89119, USA

Website:	https://workbookpress.com/
Hotline:	1-888-818-4856
Email:	admin@workbookpress.com

Ordering Information:
Quantity sales. Special discounts are available on quantity purchases by corporations, associations, and others. For details, contact the publisher at the address above.

ISBN-13:   978-1-956017-25-0 (Paperback Version)
            978-1-956017-26-7 (Digital Version)

REV. DATE: 06.30.2021

TABLE OF CONTENTS

- DEDICATION 07
- ABOUT THE AUTHOR 09
- THE DAWNING OF THE AGE 11
- MONKEY SEE, MONKEY DO 14
- HOMEBOUND, SOUTHBOUND AND DOWN 18
- THE TEEN YEARS 21
- AM I GOOD ENOUGH TO WIN OR IS SECOND PLACE GOOD ENOUGH? ... 26
- LEAVING THE NEST FOR THE COLLEGE YEARS 28
- WHERE DID THE COLLEGE CHEERLEADERS GO? 33
- THEY AWARDED ME A DEGREE TO GET RID OF ME—NOW WHAT? 37
- HOW DO YOU RESOURCE HUMANS INTO EFFECTIVE LEADERS WITH THE RIGHT WORK ETHIC? 40
- FINDING A HUSBAND AT THE SALAD BAR 42
- IS DEAD MAN DENNIS REALLY DEAD? 44
- WITHOUT DENNIS AND WITHOUT JOSEPH, WHERE WILL I FIND LOVE? 50
- RAISING MY SON AND HENRY 53
- I KNEW MY HOROSCOPE WAS CANCER, BUT I NEVER SIGNED UP TO HAVE CANCER! 56

TRICK OR TREAT COMES THE NEXT TWO YEARS	59
CAN WE JUST PUT A ZIPPER DOWN MY BELLY FOR THE NEXT 9 HOUR SURGERY?	62
GOOD HEALTH – CHECK; A NEW JOB – CHECK; SELLING THE HOUSE AND MOVING INTO MY DREAM HOME – CHECK	63
WHEN DO YOU LEAD AND WHEN DO YOU FOLLOW?	64
THE DARK DAYS OF DEPRESSION IS MORE THAN JUST A BAD HAIR DAY!!	68
ARE ONLINE DATES ONLY WHERE FROGS GO FOR LOVE?	72
AM I REALLY CRAZY OR JUST ACT THAT WAY?	78
DO YOU HAVE TO GO OUT OF TOWN TO FIND YOUR SOULMATE?	83
SHOULD WE GET MARRIED NOW THAT WE FINALLY MET?	87
WHERE DO YOU GO TO FIND PARADISE?	90
HOW DOES ONE TRAIN FOR SENIOR STATUS THAT MOST CALL ELDERLY OLD FARTS?	95
HOW DO YOU ELIMINATE LIFE'S HEARTACHES AND LIVE HAPPINESS UNTIL THE DAY WE DIE?	98
DID I TELL YOU ALL MY SECRETS?	100
A NEW DIAGNOSIS –GEOGRAPHICALLY CHALLENGED	102
AUTHOR'S GALLERY OVER THE YEARS	113

DEDICATION

I dedicate this book to friends, family, loved ones and all those that contributed to my success as I took my journey to Paradise. A special shout out to my loving son and his family, my husband and my wonderful dogs. We are ALL family.

There is yet one very special lady, Ms. Wanda, (my mom) who brought me into this world and shared laughter, tears and support. I only hope I am giving back that unconditional love for her.

I love you, Mom ♥

Kathy M. Johnson

ABOUT THE AUTHOR

A three-time cancer survivor and career woman plus a mother, most of us can relate to some components of the author's life. The trials and tribulations of divorce, near-death experiences, and the challenges of being a single woman who looks for a forever relationship offers adventure that will keep you laughing and crying as if it's your life journey.

JUNE 29, 1955 at 8:07pm...
THE DAWNING OF THE AGE

It happened and mom wasn't sure she was ready. After a near death experience with her Golden Boy which was my brother, life could never get more intense for Mom and Dad (they thought). Mom says she was 6 weeks overdue and they knocked her out for days to give birth back then. She said I made her deathly ill during the 10 ½ months of pregnancy and wondered if it was too late to change her mind; but alas, the sea parted and her little girl appeared. They named me based on the purity that they felt within me.

I guess I came out of the womb chattering. They endearingly thought of a freckled faced doll back then that talked all the time. I was nicknamed Chatty Kathy. Actually, I was rather shy in first grade due to an illness that came about at age 5. Mom used to spank me (before verbal abuse and emotional assault became popular) to go pee. Yes, I said that right. I hate to take the time to pee to this day. Why? Because unknown to everyone, including the doctors, my little internal hoes dumping out of my vertical smile that leads from the bladder to the kidneys didn't exist!

Those were the technical medical terms for it and they went in to fix the little problem which actually was a big deal back then. Dr. Travis Morgan (RIP) was a miracle doc who went in and made me a little hose/valve so that peeing came natural and I could be "normal", whatever normal is.

By the way, I still search for Normal. Back then, I found out that I was also a carrier of TB and a young boy died of TB because I infected him and didn't even know what TB was. Can you imagine growing up thinking you were a murderer and a stupid doll named "CK"? Barbie would have been better but NO! I was cute but not beautiful and my chatterbox was a coping mechanism for homeschooling in the sixth grade when Dr. Morgan had to redo his work AGAIN at age 12. Mom should have taken out the Parts Warranty when she had a chance seven years earlier. Oh Well. That wasn't all. I was always told that I was the only child that favored my Mama Grace (grandmother on dad's side).

I later found out that Mama Grace was diagnosed Paranoid Schizophrenic, Manic Depressive/multi personality and institutionalized at a very young age. Back then, they kept mental patients heavily sedated with a continuous regiment of ECT treatments, which left her basically insane and in an addictive drug induced coma state in the local mental hospital known as "Eastern State." Sorry about digressing to that "dark hole" called temporary insanity and the depression that will become my ongoing health issue for the next 60 years. There is always a happy story and a funny story to Chatty Kathy's life. Let's move forward to a pleasant memory we will call the Monkey Days.

MONKEY SEE, MONKEY DO

Have you ever gotten the feeling that nicknames really DO have a significant impact during your formative years? The old adage which I used during my bullying stage was, "sticks and stones will break my bones, but words will never hurt me." If that didn't work, I would follow by saying," I'll tell my brother and he will beat you up!" That's probably why the most-subtle, but bad, bullying actually came from my brother. Actually, he was my hero. Three years older and, I guess wiser, because he had me wrapped around his little finger.

I could walk home from grade school, only if my brother and his friends let me walk with them. Of course, that thrilled me to no end until the first day of school after band practice when my brother insisted it would be good for me to carry his trumpet along with my books. My first selected instrument was the Bells. It was huge and clumsy; and the only reason I even played an instrument was that it was required to be in the band before I could try out for Majorette. Why didn't I select the triangle or even the cymbals?

Later, upon entering high school and becoming

a Majorette, I switched to a flute. It looked like my baton, easy to carry and I could multi-task by twirling my flute! I actually made last chair but could have been first chair if the criteria were the ability to twirl my flute, not play it. The Band Director needed an office girl to answer the phone during the winter months of band. I tried out and made first chair, office staff. Now, let's go back to those wonder years. Have you ever observed a monkey playing? My next nickname as a child was Monkey face. I spent more time upside down on the monkey bars than right side up on the swing set. I hung from tree branches upside down. I figured extra blood to my brain would allow rapid growth of brain cells. I can only say that it didn't hurt.

After all, look where I would be without extra brain cells? I already was a naïve little sister and blonde, to make it worse. My brother finally quit harassing me until college after I told Mom and Nanny what he was doing by making me carry his trumpet case. Don't feel sorry for my brother. He got me back when I followed him to College and Mom no longer was available to monitor his brother behavior.

Now because I am the middle child, my kid sister really got in the line of fire when it came to cruel and unusual treatment. She had it coming. It wasn't my fault. I was 5 years older than her. Everything I did, I had to have my kid sister tag along. Now, don't feel sorry for her. She was the biggest Tattle Tale ever born. Mom still says she and Nanny witnessed me pushing my sister's stroller down the hill one day.

Does mom have eyes in the back of her head? I plead the fifth and will only say IF anything like that happened, it was an accident. Once again, Miss Tattle Tale got me back. I had just gotten my driver's license in high school and hit the ground running in Mom's Firebird. I640 was a long stretch of interstate that was new and not at all crowded.

I only wanted to see how fast that bad boy would go, so I respectfully asked Mom and Dad if I could run an errand in the Firebird. Sure, they said, as long as you take your sister! Why me? Where was my brother? Couldn't she stay home and nap or pick her nose or something? So, the kid sister is my copilot and she is 11 years old now. I told her not to tell Mom that we got the car up to 100 mph or she was dead meat.

My secret is safe with her until we pull in the driveway and out she goes to run and tattle. The real final blow was when I was riding my bike down our steep driveway one day and crashed in the gravel.

Looking down at my kneecap didn't look that bad. Lots of gravel, dirt, blood; and there a little bone showing too. MY bone was showing! Of course, little snoop dog witnessed this collision and as I ran in the back door slamming the door to the bathroom, Mom comes running, knocking on the door and asking me if I was ok. I had about 10 band aids carefully lined up like a butterfly bandage and proceeded to bite my tongue to keep from crying and screaming of pain. I'm fine; it's just a little scrape.

You got it! My sister told on me and off we go to the hospital for stitches. I guess it's true. Monkey See—Monkey Do!

HOMEBOUND, SOUTHBOUND AND DOWN

In today's environment, it is really cool to be homeschooled. But in 1968, homeschooling was dreadful. It meant my mom had to pick up daily homework assignments and bring them home. Periodically, my sixth grade teacher would pay a visit to see how I was progressing. At age 12, my little vertical smile was no longer functioning properly. When I did pee, my bladder was not emptying. One time, before the second major surgery, I was in line at the lunchroom and had to go pee. It could not wait. I had my tray in my hand and my books under my arm and before I knew it, a stream of urine puddled around my socks and shoes.

Everybody laughed and made fun. Later, when I told Mom that story, she claims she never knew that happened. I also got in trouble in the 3rd grade for answering a question for this boy during the bible verse. I got in trouble for "talking" and sent out to the hallway to stand silent while the kids came by and laughed. To this day, I still am waiting to get my day in court. Naturally, the boy didn't get in trouble; only me. Not long after that, Mom got a call from Dr. Reed, the Attila the Hun grade school principal who told mother he was sending me home for being inappropriately dressed. My dress was apparently too short.

My lace socks and patent leather white shoes were okay, but my petticoat was showing. I am sure they thought this may lead to some future career as an exhibition dancer. Back to homeschooling. After another successful plumbing surgery, I actually got invited to a dance and a party at my friend's house. It was coed!! They had great cake and ice cream and cool party favors and even prizes for special games. I didn't win anything but was having a blast being popular and fitting in with my friends.

Long about 9 pm and when the chaperones left the room, a new game were introduced. They called it "spin the bottle." After the bottle landed, you were to go into a closet with the selected victim and KISS. Kiss? Kiss what? How? Why? Do I have to? Needless, to say, that first boy kiss was short and sweet and began my love life as I know it today. It wasn't until high school that I was educated on the proper French kissing technique.

My resource document was "Everything you always wanted to know about Sex, but were afraid to Ask." Knowledge without practice does not make for excellence or even proficiency. In fact, my performance in the love category was a "low meets" at best. At that point, the diary began my passion for writing and journaling and some of my earliest secrets and confessions were behind lock and key in that little red diary...that is unless my sister found it and decided to turn me in. I really was not a bad kid, but my family thought some of my fantasies and adventures were a bit over the top.

I never skipped class and always did my homework, but I do admit whether it was out of boredom or curiosity or just plain meanness, trouble seemed to pop up from time to time. I will assure you that I was innocent. The problem is that I was a lousy liar and Mom and Dad knew that. To this day, I cannot tell a fib and get by with it. It is not in my personality and I don't have a poker face. I don't even like playing cards. You aren't supposed to talk while playing cards so I would usually just sit the card playing sessions out.

THE TEEN YEARS

The teen years are those golden years where everything happens so fast. We have new independence but still don't have to be responsible. Well, that's what I thought anyway. After the Tattle Tale ratted on me over the high speed Firebird incident, I was doomed to a life of never telling a lie. The truth was where I needed to be. I think that's where my storytelling skills began to flourish. You see white lies are still lies. But the truth, slightly embellished, still falls under the truth. Right? You just have to practice your embellishments to ensure they are believable. I have a confession to make about the story telling that can get you in trouble. First of all, this was NOT my fault. I was strongly influenced by my best friend, Diane.

Our boyfriends in high school were best of friends that went to a different high school. My boyfriend was a year older so he was college bound and no telling what kind of corruption he participated in. I worked the summer at the neighborhood community pool through two summers. There were these two cute boys from yet another local high school who asked us out. Diane, of course, was the ring leader (Sorry, Diane; I didn't mean to tell) and convinced me there would be no harm in going for a casual outing with these two guys. They invited us to the movies. Sounds innocent enough and our boyfriends were out on the town that night doing guy things anyway. So, technically, we were doing girls night out and that fell under the category of perfectly acceptable. I didn't drink back than and I was nervous.

Remember, I grew up a Baptist and my guilt was shining through even though I was innocent. Of course, that Boones Farm, Strawberry Hill the guys brought tasted like Kool aid, so what the heck. We went to the drive in. No one will see us at the drive in. So, I didn't exactly tell Mom and Dad and of course not Miss Tattle Tale or Brother Bully, because that would have great information to casually pass on so I could get in trouble.

Confucius say: those who play will pay. What the heck did that mean? Sunday after church was particularly tense because Diane and I had to make sure our stories were the same in case we got separated. I guess you need to know what happened so here goes. Boones Farm by the bottle with a straw is not recommended. I was sitting up front and my guy friend got out of the car to hit the bathroom. When he got the driver's side door opened, I accidentally fell over where the door handle was and split my head open.

Unknown to me, there was no pain but blood was dripping and when I turned around to speak to Diane and the other guy in the back, they screamed. What? What? Did you see someone we knew? OMG...we couldn't go to the hospital for stitches. Our boyfriends would cover for us but we couldn't tell them the whole truth and nothing but the truth. God forbid by Monday; my siblings would hear the gossip at school.

Mom would be outraged and use the big stick, "wait till your father gets home." We quickly wiped away the blood. It didn't need stitches, right? A butterfly bandage would work. Yes, I will quickly run home and sneak in the bathroom where my Band-Aid stash was and proceed to conduct surgery on my eye before anyone woke up or Mom saw me with the eyes in back of her head. Not only did my own blood turn my stomach but the Boones Farm didn't exactly wash down the nasty hot dog I ate at the drive in.

So, here we go, back to my house to sneak in, get to the bathroom before puking my guts up and therefore have a lot of explaining to do. If I got away with my sin that night, Diane and I still had Sunday to (1) show up for church; (2) justify the big bruise where I hit my head and last but not least, concoct the story that would be true, but slightly embellished, to save face with the boyfriends.

What a weekend! Sunday afternoon came and here come our boyfriends to the house. "How was your evening, boys?" Good. How was yours?" Just ok. What happened to your eye, "Chatty Kathy"? "Oh, that", I said. Diane and I were out at night practicing our baton routine when down came a branch and hit me on the head.

We had gone to the movies and come home early. Really? What movie? (Oh, No!!!!!! We forgot to rehearse that part.) "Diane, what was the name of the movie again?" The only person worse at telling a fib than me was her. Her tale kept getting worse and worse until finally the guys said they knew the truth!!! I didn't know if that was a bluff or not, so I was laying low with my poker face and no eye contact.

We would have pulled it off if Diane had not have said, "I knew they wouldn't believe it, "Chatty Kathy"!!!" At that moment, ole Hawkeyes in the back of her head interrupted to say, "What happened to your eye, "Chatty Kathy"?" I simply stood up and said, "you all wouldn't believe it if I told you." Rats! Busted; and I didn't even have to true confess. But the storytelling part was a lot of fun and if I had told the whole truth and nothing but the truth, they would not have believed me and I could go about my business. Oh Well. Another "CK"ism: Start growing eyes in the back of your head so you will be ready when your own child is born. I remembered that and began working on my witchcraft techniques right away.

AM I GOOD ENOUGH TO WIN OR IS SECOND PLACE GOOD ENOUGH?

I began dancing at the age of two and my happy feet performed on stage every year from age two until twenty-two. Actually, I still have happy feet but need to cultivate some happy moves on the dance floor with hubby. It's a work in progress. Love that man but trying to teach Bobby to shag is like teaching a Nuclear Physicist the crash technical training course on Radiation. What's the point? In high school, there was a test (the guidance counselor called it an evaluation since you can't test proficiency in a teenager that has a priority of what outfit will look the best for the dance and what shall we do after the Friday football game.) Those are top priority.

You see, I am a trainer by trade but early on saw a love for education, psychology, the arts, public speaking, English, and animals. My career path and advanced education touched on many of those passions. Writing, of course, was already a work in progress since my first diary was created in the 6th grade. Anyway, the Strong-Campbell Skills Assessment was an excellent tool to determine was kind of qualities one should move toward based on how you answer a series of life questions. Was I going to be a Doctor, Lawyer or Indian Chief? How about a Missionary, a Veterinarian or Mother Teresa? Some kids were identified as future lawyers, politicians (those are the ones that cheated on the test, no doubt) or even a successful businessman? Nope.

My destiny was Funeral Director. You have to admit the market and supply and demand will always exist. Actually, I did consider Funeral Director when I later became everyone's Executor of Wills, writer of the best obituaries (See Dead Man Dennis chapter down the road), as well as an exemplary party planner which they no long call a wake, funeral, or party. They are now called a Celebration of Life.

I wrote and spoke eulogies. I planned where to spread ashes and even took the lead on spreading several family members, friends, loved ones, dogs and even an ex-husband. I know what you are thinking. I disposed of his ashes, but I did NOT kill him. That IS the truth and nothing but the truth. AMEN as a trainer by trade, I am passionate about lifelong learning and the more skill sets, the better. By the way, there are more nicknames forthcoming that hint at future skill sets I became proficient in and quite infamous at performing. (Magic "CK", Ginger Rogers, the Fortune Teller, and untiring romantic.) Stay tuned for further development.

LEAVING THE NEST FOR THE COLLEGE YEARS

Highschool was so much fun that I was sure nothing could top those wonder years. So many memories from high school left me very lost in many ways to imagine leaving my hometown to travel 100 miles south to Chattanooga, TN. I had motivation for going away to college. The University was not that far away so that when I ran out of beer money (I meant money for food), I could commute back home. It was very lonely my freshman year. I only knew one person and that was bully brother. But I made majorette and joined a sorority and got a roommate named Gail. This was a walking campus back in the day and it was easy to get involved. I also got a part time job at the School of Business to have extra spending money.

Mom and Dad said they would fund my higher education as long as I went to class and didn't flunk out or get put in jail. Who me? I studied at the local beer joint which was, the dive that had the coldest beverages and the best hamburgers. I got another nickname from my roommate. She named me Spud. When she had a wee bit too much adult beverage, Spud became "Spuddy Buddy." Our sorority was the best. The sorority house was also walking distance from the School of Business and a half a block from ALL the fraternity houses.

I even was selected by a fraternity to be their "little sister." Do you know what qualifies you for the honor of little sister? I didn't either except I was supposed to be a magnet during rush week to get the best of the best guys to join the fraternity. Their fraternity house was so much like Animal House. In fact, in addition to being the magnet, we were also assigned to clean up the house on Sunday afternoon. Nasty beer cans were thrown up against the wall into a garbage can that was a make shift basketball goal.

I won't gross you out about the cleanup of the Passion Pit. Let's just say, I refused the role of maid and told them I will give them an extra dose of cuteness during pledge week. They agreed. They also loved it that I was a part time secretary in the School of Business. If I wasn't such a prude, I could have had a wonderful side business making copies of the tests that I typed and reproduced for the professors.

To be clear, I never cheated and there was never any pressure to do so. I also secretly wanted to date a jock and never could figure out why the Head Majorette could not land a date with a football jock.

My high school squeeze got tired of the long distance relationship every weekend and stayed back home at the local University. I began to date another sports jock which was the pitcher on the baseball team. Lee was so sweet and he never had that bad boy image. I have to confess being a baseball widow girlfriend was not that exciting. Lee and I finally drifted apart too.

    A few football guys courted me and that was kind of exciting. One was on the Offense and the other was a Defensive player. This little story brings back a lot of anxiety and confirms how mean brother bully can be. My brother and now sister-in-law were college sweethearts and they would often come and sit on the wall outside the girl's dorm at night. Well, one day someone stole my wallet with all my money in it. What would I do for food? What would I do for my sorority dues? How would I buy my books? Who in hell would spot me for beer money? Surely my brother would be concerned for his sweet sister.

    I told my brother the dilemma and he flipped me a quarter. I said, "What's that for?" He shouted and laughed, "Go call someone that gives a damn!!" I did. I called home. He was in trouble now. One time my Offensive football guy took me to dinner. But I forgot that Mr. Defense asked me out for a nightcap the same night. Oh dear!!! I can't hurt anyone's feelings and besides, I was still trying to decide which was better in life—offense from Alabama or defense from New York? Mr. Offense and I ate dinner but before the check came, I suddenly came down with a bug that forced my guy to take me back to the dorm early.

My brother and his girlfriend were having their evening wall date and he spoke to Offense when we returned to the dorm. My brother inquired about me not feeling well. A quick kiss on the cheek and off I went. I had only a half hour to get better, change clothes and be ready for Round Two. (Ladies: you cannot tell me this never happened to you.) So, Mr. Defense arrives and speaks to them, and said he was there to pick up his kid sister.

Oh really, brother said, you may not want to take her out. She is feeling bad this evening." Out I came skipping merrily with open arms. BUSTED!! After he quit laughing and by Monday back at the wall, brother begins to lecture me about dating the Offense and the Defense at the same time! He said there were fights in the locker room and I needed to back off! I told him he would protect me.

His nickname was Chop because he was a serious

black belt in karate. Many years later at homecoming with a friend from our College, I found out from tailgating with the football jock alums that they wanted to ask me out, but knew what Chop Chop would do to them if they were out of line. WHAT???? He completely shut down my social life in college and I never knew it. I told Mom and Dad what he had done, looking for sympathy.

Dad said he had an agreement with my big brother to "protect" me from bad boys that would do me wrong. Mom laughed and said it was a ploy to keep me being a good girl and preventing me from majoring in fun instead of business and psychology. Once again, I get no respect! No worries, I will get revenge sometime, someway.

WHERE DID THE COLLEGE CHEERLEADERS GO?

You won't believe me when I tell you about my "best and final" husband. He is the love of my life. He is from my past and I never knew it. By the way, you will hear more about the two previous husbands later. It took me kissing a lot of frogs over the years to find my best and final hubby, when he was right under my nose at the same college. I will keep you in suspense a little longer but Best Buddy Bobby remembered me from college since he was a college cheerleader, body builder, runner, hiker, bartender, adventurer, and in general a piece of work.

The piece of work part comes as testimony from his friends and family. Stay tuned for his future publication if you think my life stories were fun. Chatty's life is that of a nun compared to hubbys' ventures. I found it ironic that GBS was his initials. BS? Bobby does not have a bull s**t bone in his body. (If you believe that, we both have a nice piece of property in the ocean to sell you!) By the way, he is over my shoulder, as we speak, insisting that all photos and reference to him must be reviewed and approved BEFORE I publish.

Hey, buster, go write your own book! I am on a roll! Remember folks, my disclaimer is that all stories are true, slightly embellished perhaps, but I do not tell lies. If you don't believe that, ask Mom. She will tell you when I am telling a fib. Meanwhile, back to how my advanced studies led me to my eventual career path and passions. No, not a Funeral Director. That might come later. I wanted to be a Special Education major with a concentration on working with autistic children.

I figured I could counsel my young patients by talking nonstop until they act out and scream out in frustration, I would break their tormented silence and all would be good. The problem was science and math. I had no idea how much science was required for Special Educators. Biology and Chemistry were not my strong suit and although I wasn't a bad mathematician, I never saw the point of Algebra and Geometry.

In freshman Biology lab, I couldn't even prick my own finger to test for blood type, which is ironic since I now prick my finger twice daily due to Type II Diabetes. So knowing if I can't handle seeing my own blood, I surely would not be able to pull off the rest of my Science lab requirements. Walking out of biology class and walking back to the dorm one day,

I was asking God to give me a sign of what my destiny would be. I got to the top of the hill and looked to the left (the School of Business) and looked to the right (the Psychology Department) and thought, I will try both and go from there. I also landed that secretary job in the School of Business, so my decision was made.

A major in Business Administration with emphasis in Office Management and a minor in Psychology was my future career choice. My post graduate degree at the Masters level, by the way, was completed back at the local University in Technological and Adult Education with an emphasis in Performance Based Training. Post grad studies got me to all but dissertation (ABD) in Counseling Psychology with emphasis in troubled children's therapy.

When it got to the dissertation part, I decided to just write a book which would hopefully be a lot more interesting than some bible size document of boring research that probably would not conclude much. My dissertation by the way was centered on Executive Leadership. So you see, although I went from down the hill to up the hill to over the hill, everything I am passionate about fell naturally into place.

By the way, I still hate seeing my own blood and pricking my finger. It is what it is, I guess. Life is all good and it sure beats the alternative. As a 3-time Cancer survivor of 15 years, I can tell you near death experiences will leave you with a much different attitude about the importance of life. God either keeps you on earth as a work in progress with nine lives; or knocking at the pearly gates ready to join my other angelic family, friends, and dogs combined with a mixed bag of those that get forgiveness before the BIG DAY. I reserved my seat in heaven long ago and hope the tickets don't expire for at least another 40 years.

THEY AWARDED ME A DEGREE TO GET RID OF ME—NOW WHAT?

After graduating, I began to visualize what the real world would look like. Where do I belong? I broke an engagement with the baseball player, had no room back home since my sister took over my room, and had no money to venture out on my own. I had no real love life and no place to live. The sky and location to live were for me to find. I got an interview in Atlanta with a Law Firm to be their executive administrator for the Firm. The Senior Administrative Supervisor didn't like this snotty nosed college brat. She offered me the job at entry level making barely more than the midnight shift bag lady at the grocery store. I decided to migrate home to Knoxville, TN.

By the way, my future best buddy and hubby was in another committed marriage and working in guess where? Yes, he was in Atlanta and I was going the opposite direction. I tell you it's serendipity. I am sure we passed on the interstate, stood in line to get gas at the same station; and who knows, he may have bought me drink somewhere through the years and I had forgotten. You just never know. Only time will tell. Fast forward from 1977 – 2013 and God decided we were ready for each other. Meanwhile, I took a job offer in Knoxville at a major Real Estate firm and stayed for one year until two twin brothers came to town to buy property and begin West Knoxville's first small animal hospital.

They grew up in Iowa and started their practice in Miami, Florida where nice old ladies spend more on their pets than on their spouses and children. For $100.00 per month more, they recruited me to be their girl Friday. I set up accounting books, helped in surgery, cared for the pets in ICU, gave fluids, coordinated Nurf basketball tournaments when we had no clients and painted benches for the waiting room. Another year of the ideal job passed until I was awarded a Q clearance and was swept away to Oak Ridge, TN where I would spend the rest of my work time in the Human Resources field at and around a weapons plant (Y12).

The Plant was the very place where the A-bomb was fabricated during the Manhattan Project. My Dad worked on that project of national importance and he never knew it was the A Bomb until it was detonated and the War ended. Wow, what rich national security secrets we were involved in. It's a good thing the White House did not have access to our communication devices and thank God, social media didn't exist. I won't give you my opinion of politics and current events. Ask others if you want to hear what is best for the USA. This is honestly the first time in 61 years that I am fearful about the status of our free country. But I get one vote in a couple of months and I am sure Americans will wise up about our Commander in Chief. Enough said.

HOW DO YOU RESOURCE HUMANS INTO EFFECTIVE LEADERS WITH THE RIGHT WORK ETHIC?

It has taken me 30 years to understand humans in the workplace and I still question whether Executives understand the difference between management and leadership. I became a student of Steven Covey, Tom Peters, Kepner-Tregoe, Edward Deming, Learning as Leadership, Certifications in Human Resources, advanced degrees, the school of hard knocks and on the job training. I think I learned more from my mistakes and what not to do as a Manager than all the book learning and awards I received when I got it right. Cancer kind of stopped me in my tracks some 18 years ago when I got religion and made my priority living rather than climbing the ladder until I banged my head on the corporate glass ceiling.

By the way, I do not regret subtle discriminations and radiation exposure all those years. It showed me that when you deal with human beings that are not always trustworthy or have a superior work ethic, you learn that life is really too short to sweat the small stuff. It's all small stuff when you fight for your life. That which does not kill us truly does make us stronger and different in many ways. But as my career matured with skills both in life and work, I created many CKisms. Food for thought goes something like this: I say if you fight with pigs, you will get down and dirty in the mud and no one wins.

In other words, pick your friends and colleagues and mentors carefully. Some folks are working the same agenda. Some of them work their own agenda and will drag anyone in their way down on the ground. Moral of the story is watch out for the pigs! They come in all colors, shapes and sizes.

If you aren't careful, you will get caught in the cross fire of their drama and end up bearing the burden. Trust me—been there, done that. Don't be naive and when you think utopia in your job has finally been accomplished, wait until tomorrow. That too will change. Your job is always a work in progress.

FINDING A HUSBAND AT THE SALAD BAR

The salad bar at work is where I finally looked. I tried being a barfly and kissing a few tadpoles, but most were either a kissing cousin, someone that was separated (Call me when the ink is dry, buddy), or someone's ex-husband carrying all kinds of past sins. There are always two sides to every story; her version, his version and the real story. Also, be careful when you are 25 and single to avoid raising someone else's kid from a previous marriage. If I was going to raise kids, it would be my own puppies. Blended families carry lots of drama. Mom actually introduced me to dead man Dennis.

Dennis was a computer programmer at the bomb plant. We dated for a year with a few ups and downs and decided to marry April 26, 1980. Little Jason arrived on the scene July 7, 1983 and he deserves a chapter of his own later on. My son was the legacy I was given from my 10-year marriage; and I truly won the prize. Dennis, after divorce, became an absentee dad and owed my son $10,000 dollars in back child support at the time of his death in 2001. Don't feel sorry for Dennis. He pickled his liver with alcohol while in his third marriage. I had to have him cremated and disposed of respectfully, out of respect for Jason. (See the Dead Man Dennis chapter and remember, I DID NOT kill him. But I did bury him. It was the right thing to do, even though it cost me another $5,000 in the end. Don't feel sorry for me at this point. I will tell you that the Good Lord made Dennis' financial debt even upon his death. Stay tuned. Karma does really happen.

IS DEAD MAN DENNIS REALLY DEAD?

Please do not judge me as I tell you about my first husband, Dennis. He passed away from alcoholism. I do not tell this story to be disrespectful. He is the father of my son and for the first 5 years of Jason's life, he was a good dad. I think my son would agree. No matter what, he was still his dad and I tried to raise our son to show respect for people unless they try to harm you physically, emotionally and/or mentally. My marriage to Dennis was 5 years of bliss and 5 years of living hell. Two things happened to Dennis that were show stoppers to our marriage. One was the bottle and the other was that he died at age 50 of alcoholism.

He was on his third marriage. Our divorce was final in 1990 after a most traumatic incident when Dennis struck me, as alcohol influenced his personality and anger. I told him when we began dating that if a man abused a woman physically, emotionally and/or mentally, they better be ready for the consequences. Dennis broke all three and divorce became my significant emotional event that left a big scar on my heart, making at chance at a loving relationship a very vulnerable experience. Over the years, I have been single longer than I was married. Independent and self-sufficient were two words that I perfected.

Submissive was not in my vocabulary. Some men friends over the years explained to me that I intimidated a man when trying to get to know me. If so, I was destined to be single a lot longer. If it meant the midnight nurse would be holding my hand when I took my last breath, I was willing to opt for alone over a dysfunctional and toxic relationship.

So, in August 1990, I began to date a gentleman named Joseph. Was he really gentleman Joseph, rebound Will or the love of my life? Joseph and I were together for 5 years and I still believe those 5 years were some of the best. The problem was age. No, I wasn't a Cougar; in fact, he was 18 years older than me. We worked together at the plant but never really knew each other since I was married and he was single; and I have this rule that if you are in an exclusive committed relationship, you stay faithful unless someone breaks that exclusiveness.

Joseph was what I needed at the time. During that relationship period, my son was seven years old and I was in a stressful management position and starting over after the divorce. I took Jason and left the family home with most of the furniture behind with Dennis. I started renting places. I tried to respect Dennis as a parent with joint custody, even though he eventually was an absentee father. I really didn't mind as long as he honored the court decision on child support and he was responsible when he had our son. Those two rules he broke as well. He was always in arrears on child support and he forgot to pick up and drop off our son at the scheduled time. He forced me to have Jason become a latch key kid, even though I was usually at home when he was to drop him off. He was always late and one could imagine the anxiety that is created when your child is missing.

My son's guidance counselor in school appointed him to be the President of the Banana Splits group. That was the term for "broken" families who were divorced. Although pretty discriminating, the Banana Split counselor taught very important lessons. The first one was never get in a car if mommy or daddy are driving and drinking beer or other alcoholic beverage. Jason refused to go with his dad one time because of an open beer and he was sure I was badmouthing him in front of our son. I didn't have to.

The school system supported that notion and I am so glad. When Jason became of age, we talked about drinking and driving and drinking in moderation.

He explained to me that he had seen the ugly side of alcohol abuse and I believe that was a very good lesson we all should have learned over the years. One day long after my divorce to Dennis, I was contacted at work by someone I never met. Out of the clear blue, the phone rang at work and a woman asked me if I was "Chatty Kathy".

When you work in a weapon's facility, you learn to question those you don't know and this was one of them. "Who wants to know?" I asked. "Well this is Betty, she said, and Dennis is dead!!!! Since you were wife number two and he was the father of your son, I thought you would want to know." OMG—what happened? When is the funeral? Where was he? She said he could rot in the morgue as far as she was concerned! She kicked him out and the maids found his body at a cheap motel where he was living. He left her with no money and he was fired from his job. She got a beat up car with a trunk full of beer cans. She said if I wanted his body, she would gladly release it.

They lived in Florida and we lived in Tennessee. I wrote the obituary, paid money to have him cremated, and told my son we would have his ashes shipped up to our home out of respect for his father. So you see, Dennis had drunk himself to death two days before the Countries 9-11 tragedy, at age 50 with nothing left but debt and a $10,000 back child support statement. I tried to contact his first wife to notify his daughter of his death, but her husband would not let me give her details and he said he would let his wife tell their daughter, if she wanted.

To this day, I am not sure if she knew of her father's death. After their divorce, he left her with back child support and he was an absentee dad when they ended their marriage some 5 years before we met. It should have been a sign. His body was cremated and would be delivered to my door. On Saturday evening, my friends were over for a get together and the doorbell rang. It was Fed Ex, delivering a package from Florida. You guessed it. My friends asked who was at the door since we weren't expecting anyone else. I presented Dennis in a box and for the last time, he joined in the party.

Later that evening as people began to depart, I realized I was going to be alone with a dead man in a box that wasn't even invited to the party. Two friends were so kind to volunteer to help me dispose of Dennis, so off we went to find his final destiny. You must realize that Dennis had no living relatives, a daughter that could care less, and Jason was more worried about my grieving than his own. Dennis. at the end of our marriage. was a professed atheist and

I had spent $5,000 on a proper cremation.

The only thing I knew to do was spread those ashes in a place where I last knew him—close to his work in a radioactive infested section of the lake. Of course, I did not have a permit to dispose but after all the water already glowed so what's one more pile of debris. Rest Well, Dennis, wherever you are.

My son had said his goodbyes to his dad long before his death and we never really discussed the pain of losing someone you loved. Life went on for us, but not without many near death experiences for me. By this time, I was diagnosed with a rare Cancer that became my living hell from 1999, 2000 and 2001.

WITHOUT DENNIS AND WITHOUT JOSEPH, WHERE WILL I FIND LOVE?

There were a couple of other long term relationships that followed my relationship with Joseph, but honestly, by this time, I was so fearful of toxic relationships that I tended to close them down if everything didn't feel just right. Several gentlemen following the Joseph relationship were in fact 2-5 years in duration, but these gentlemen did not want to raise someone else's kid and I get that. It was always the first discussion that occurred.

My number one priority will always be my son until he begins his own family some day and doesn't need the constant guidance and support from his number one fan; and that was his mom. I truly understood that idea because, after all, I wasn't too keen on raising someone else's kid either. I tended to be attracted to older gentlemen that already had raised their kids and wanted a more flexible lifestyle, void of soccer mom, karate tournaments, birthday parties, indoor soccer, school soccer and club soccer; dances, errands, school homework and the likes of Jason and his buddies hanging around.

Personally, I would like to consider myself one of the "cool" moms and my son's friends would often hang out at our house for fun on the weekends. Not that being a single mom, with a full time career, wasn't a challenge. In fact, now that I am retired, I don't see how I multitasked and still had energy at the end of the day to cultivate any relationship.

So where does a single gal with a busy life find a healthy and loving relationship? I tried being a bar fly, but bars are not the recommended site for searching for the good ones in a pool full of bad and ugly ones. I am a social butterfly so meeting and greeting new friends were something that always came naturally. See, something does come out of extraverted personality types. I tried church too.

That's when I picked one and married a fine church going person that I knew from years earlier at work. Hubby number two was a nice guy but so totally opposite. No offense to hubby number two. We lasted less than two years. In hindsight, I was lonely and the time had come to let go of the apron strings, as Jason had convinced me that the fraternity house on campus should be his new bachelor pad when entering college.

It was only a 20-minute commute to campus. Jason embellished the positives on behalf of such a move by explaining how difficult it was to find parking and if he was on campus, he could walk to class, study at the library and participate in study groups with his friends and fellow students. He even presented a cost benefit analysis, complete with total cost savings that he/we could incur as a result of moving on campus. Work was pretty much on automatic pilot and frankly, life was steady state, until 1999. Cancer hit the first time in 1999 with follow-up near death surgeries in 2000 and 2001. I will discuss the Cancer story in a bit more detail coming in later chapters.

RAISING MY SON AND HENRY

You thought I had an only child. I did, but Henry was a necessary addition to the family. My dad had passed away in 1995. Shortly after, I decided what would complete our little family was a beautiful Golden Retriever puppy named Henry Alexander. I named him Henry in memory of dad. People that knew him call my dad Kirk, AK, buddy by his sisters, and other names over the years that I am sure I should not mention.

To me, he was Dad. Anyway, Henry was so expressive when I would have one-on-one conversations with Henry, he would look at me as if he had known me for years. I don't believe in reincarnation necessarily, but that dog seemed to get into things, as if he knew more than what a normal dog's intellect could offer. Henry flunked out of obedience school. Henry ran away and ended up sitting in cement at a construction site.

He came home with the worst constipation you could imagine. He had to have his own baby pool that he would sit in constantly even when it rained. He would greet me at the back door of our fenced in back yard, covered in mud. If you didn't know better, you would have thought he was a chocolate lab. He thought he was a lap dog. I should have named him Marley and had him audition for the sequel to the Marley and Me movie. Henry was a piece of work.

When we built our dream house, he refused to exist in a zero lot lined yard, so a friend had a retired family with a huge farm that Henry and his toys and his clothes and his baby pool went to. It was kind of like Henry outgrew me and he too wanted to start his own farm life where he could romp and stomp all he wanted. Another memory was Jason learned how to swing dance in our kitchen before the Junior-Senior prom.

He thought it was stupid at the time, until his date and her girlfriends discovered his 'Dancing with the Stars' talent. He ran in the house that night of the dance to wake me up and tell me he was the star of the dance. It appears that his dance card kept him on the dance floor with all the girls who dreamed of shagging on the beach, under the boardwalk. His lovely bride later told me that Jason's dancing ability was one of the best lessons I ever taught him, among other attributes and manners that hopefully stuck.

While under my roof, that young man knew how to sort and do laundry as well as faithfully make his bed up daily. He helped me in the kitchen with cooking and he got his first job at 15 at the local golf and country club that we belonged to. He worked in the pro shop and became a pretty good golfer as well as learning the fine art of customer service. I bought his first car and he wanted to trade up about two years. So, I signed over the title and said if he could get someone to loan him more money, he could make that decision himself.

He presented his case and, sure enough, a bank gave him a loan that would become his first experience at living paycheck to paycheck and staying in debt. Welcome to the real world! Fast forward to the fall of 1999...

I KNEW MY HOROSCOPE WAS CANCER, BUT I NEVER SIGNED UP TO HAVE CANCER!

It was 1999 when I kept having a urinary tract infection that wouldn't clear up. I was very aware of the vulnerabilities of my weak bladder. In the back of my mind, I wandered if history was repeating itself from age 5 and age 12, when my bladder repair was more than minor surgery and recovery. I walked in to my long time primary care doctor, Charlie, and he took one look at me and said, "Jump up on the table and drop your drawers." Something seems wrong. Jumping up on the table and saddling up to the stirrups for a vaginal exam was routine by this time.

Dropping my drawers was not a come on and besides, Charlie saw more of my body inside and out. But he saw something different in my eyes and between my legs as well. It was around Halloween of 1999 and I wasn't interested in trick or treats. Charlie later admitted he thought it looked like advanced Ovarian Cancer and I would be a goner by Christmas. He called my Gynecologist, and I was scheduled for emergency surgery two days later. The doctor asked me if I was through having kids because a hysterectomy should fix me up for good.

At age 37, terminating painful periods was a God send. Yes, let's do it! What should have taken 45 minutes, took 5 hours of surgery. When the doctor opened me up, tumor masses like clusters of grapes covered my vital organs! Some were benign and others were already malignant. My mom panicked when the doctor kept sending word out to mom in the hospital waiting room that she found Cancer.

A complete hysterectomy was required and careful dissection of tumors peeled off my organs. The prognosis looked bad. She had seen this rare Cancer at Emory University when she was doing her residency. That was the good news. The bad news was LPD (disseminated leiomyomatosis peritonitis) only occurred at that time in just 100 reported cases in the Country and all but me were usually in their 3rd trimester of pregnancy where hormones were raging. LPD tumors would breed off of estrogen and at 37 years of age, I came out of surgery minus female body parts and full blown menopause, with no hope of ever having hormones in my body to minimize the craziness of menopause.

Chemotherapy and radiation were not options. Thank goodness, because today I would graciously decline the toxic side effects of such therapy. Instead, a steroid called Lupron was successfully used in reported cases of other LPD patients. I called them "butt shots" because it was injected in my hip biweekly and boy, did it hurt. Of course, it beat the alternative. Life took on a different meaning in 1999-2001.

TRICK OR TREAT COMES THE NEXT TWO YEARS

Did Lupron and constant CAT scans prevent LPD from reentering my body? At the annual recheck, my doctor discovered it was back and twice as bad. The doctor didn't know where to go from there. "Chatty Kathy" felt like making a sign and walking the streets in search for another Cancer surgeon to take my case. By December, I got word from the head of Oncology at Vanderbilt Hospital. The good doctor would take my case.

Research began and by January, I traveled to Nashville, TN to a conference room full of the medical team, to discuss the process I was about to go through. I worked in Oak Ridge, TN, and my friends in the Biology Division and Life Sciences Division took it upon themselves to educate me on LPD and its causes. Why did it come back and twice as bad? I was ready to listen to the medical team, researchers, and books and of course, and anything I could personally get my hands on through the internet. I was headed to 9 hours of serious surgery to fight this monster called CANCER. Stress, like tragedy always seems to come in 3s and I was no exception.

Prior to surgery, I was notified by my boss that I was on the layoff list and would have to terminate. I never questioned (why me?) about my illness, but terminated?? I was rated as an exemplary employee. I was 8 years away from being able to retire with full pension. I was the only one in Human Resources at ORNL that had to go that year. In addition, I was selling my home and building my dream home.

Can you imagine having Cancer, having no job, having a child going off to college with college tuition and all the expenses incurred and a double mortgage if my home did not sell? Don't forget, I was a single parent with an ex-husband behind on child support. I once again turned to prayer and asked God to give me a sign.

Which part of my life do I worry about first? The answer became clear. Worry about your health and the rest will work itself out. I took short term disability and a year sabbatical to find other job opportunities, and God gave me another chance at life. Indeed, he did, for I survived the 9 hours of surgery with all of the cancer cells surgically removed again. This time more tumor masses were malignant. My doctor put me on a very strong steroid called Megace.

As I understood it, Megace was often used in

advanced Cancer patients who would quit eating and be ready to die. If I know what I know now about Megace, I would pass on that therapy prevention. Megace left my body very toxic. I had that moon face look. My hormones were raging and I gained 95 pounds, which led me to being diagnosed as a Type II Diabetic, to name a few health dilemmas. Megace worked in spite of what it did to my body, until Halloween 2001.

CAN WE JUST PUT A ZIPPER DOWN MY BELLY FOR THE NEXT 9 HOUR SURGERY?

I won't bore you with the outcome of number three. Sometimes in my life, the third time is a charm. Doc discussed a real possibility of impacting my bladder and what might be required, which was "bagging me off". A colostomy was not on my wish list. Prayer took me through the best and final living hell of more 9-hour surgery. My doctor, the hero, rushed me into recovery right when Mom came in. I looked at Mom with crocodile tears and asked, "What did I get?" She knew what I meant and as if I were age 5 all over again, she shouted, he got it all! I knew what she meant.

The team of doctors and God had given me yet another shot at life on earth. Six weeks and a CAT scan took me back to Nashville and I begged my doctor to take me off of Megace. He was very cautious but finally agreed that quality of life was more important at this point. Three months later, I dropped 65 pounds without even trying and by June, I dropped another 25 pounds. I could not have felt better.

GOOD HEALTH – CHECK; A NEW JOB – CHECK; SELLING THE HOUSE AND MOVING INTO MY DREAM HOME – CHECK

Life was good. But stress still existed. Lots of bills and still in constant therapy for lifestyle changes. The new job was very high stress as a Human Resource Director of a Waste Management contractor. My staff consisted of two employees. I frankly was used to staffs of 10-100 in the peak of my training director career with the Department of Energy facilities. I was operating with two employees and myself. A year passed; and I quit with the possibility of contract work with a consulting firm in Oak Ridge, TN.

The first month consulting, I secured a major contract with a firm out of Erwin, Tennessee. The president of the firm offered me a partnership role as Vice President of Strategic Planning and Business Development. I was finally doing work I was passionate about and coined the phrase, "I would do this for free if someone would pay my mortgage. Life was good. Now what?

WHEN DO YOU LEAD AND WHEN DO YOU FOLLOW?

Are those the only choices in life? My choice is to lead as opposed to manage. Remember, I have advanced studies in the area of Executive Leadership and Team building. (Not to mention trial and error). I was a consultant for many years coaching top level executives from supervisors to plant managers to CEOs. My employer in Oak Ridge afforded me the opportunity to work with strategic planning groups, key executives in government as well as nonprofits and profit organizations. Those were some sweet memories and downright "knock your socks off" assignments.

I facilitated strategic planning, team building off sites, rational problem solving-decision making analysis sessions and one on one coaching with some pretty high level individuals. A few that I will never forget dealt with problem solving issues with the Under Secretary of the Department of Energy and his team of executives. They flew me to Washington, DC to meet the head guys in the Department of Energy. I won't go into detail since you don't talk about the outcomes of such high level sessions.

Another challenging assignment was with the Defense Logistics Agency with the Department of Defense. A little closer to home, I had a great 5-year contract with the Tennessee Department of Transportation (TDOT) as an Executive Leadership Development Coach. Traveling to Nashville was a joy since my son and his family live there. Nashville is also my home away from home at Vanderbilt Hospital.

So, no matter what, I will continue to visit my home state. I do miss Tennessee at times and tonight is the first University of Tennessee football game on TV. We would watch it in a sports bar down here; but there are those Florida gators fans everywhere and they love to hate Tennessee every chance they get. No matter what, I proudly wear my Orange and White every Saturday and cheer my team on. When we aren't watching and going to my home town for football games, my hubby and I go back to our alma mater every chance we get.

Homecoming is a time to reconnect with dear friends who cheered, win or lose, for our college football team. My son and daughter-in-law are also graduates of my hometown University, so when fall arrives, we all bring out our Orange and White. Good times and great memories. Hubby and I have stayed in touch with a lot of old friends from our alma mater and it's like we never missed a day together. The good ole days will never be replaced.

After College awarded me with a BS in Business Administration and a minor in Psychology, I later continued my post graduate education in at my hometown University, where I earned a MS in Technological and Adult Education. Further studies in Counseling Psychology got me to all but dissertation when I decided this book would be more fun than researching some boring theory that no one but my professors would read. In fact, my business partner, gave me a copy of his dissertation from his PhD program. No offense, but this book might be an easier read for most.

Some of the theory and the words you wrote were over most people's head. I have high regards for my business partner and his intellect. Being a principle of our consulting firm, was the best of times in the world of work for me. If only the year 2008 economy hadn't happened, we would still be working away solving the world's human resources problems. At the time we closed the doors, I was marrying off my son, getting a divorce, dealing with the after math of Cancer and suddenly unemployed!

Over the years, one can see why I believe that what does not kill us, makes us stronger. I never had minor setbacks. They always came in threes, sometimes more. It made me a better person, actually. I sure didn't believe that at the time of chaos in my life. But overcoming stress, anxiety, and depression has become a way of life for me.

THE DARK DAYS OF DEPRESSION IS MORE THAN JUST A BAD HAIR DAY!!

I get so tired of family, friends, psychologists and shrinks saying when my depression struck, "well, "Chatty Kathy" you don't look sick. JUST GET OVER IT!!! Unless you want to deal with consequences, never tell a person with mental illness issues to just get over it. It's not like a normal healthy person when you wake up and have a bad hair day. It is more than a sick feeling after binge drinking in college when you are hung over and vow to never drink again. No, it's the dark hole without lights and without a rope to rescue you.

The depressed person can scream all you want but it's like, "why bother." No one is able to rescue you from darkness and take the pain away. The stigma of mental illness is why I became so interested in Psychology. There is nothing more fascinating than the human mind. One flew over the Cuckoo's Nest is actually pretty close to the mental institutions around town. A psychiatrist will pop another pill of psych drugs to add to the already pile of pill cocktail that you already consume.

If you can't sleep, there is a pill for that. Mood swings are no problem. There are plenty of pills for that. Have a panic attack and you get another pill? Depression has an entire book of fun pills from Zanax to Prozac to Seroquel and even Lithium and Haldol. Haldol is what they give Alzheimer patients to turn them into vegetables with zero expressions, emotions, and life. A shrink put me on Haldol one time and I begged him to give me my smile and personality back.

With Psych drugs, you can put your "game face" on and most people still see my everything is beautiful personality. At the same time, your guts feel like they are on fire and you are sure you must be carrying 150 pound weights on your shoulders. All you want to do is sleep, hide under the covers all day and pretend you only exist in the world and cry—sometimes uncontrollably. But most of the time, those dark days are spent alone with the blinds shut and isolated from the outside world. No one but my faithful hound dog, Molly was tolerable.

I loved Molly more than myself many times. She literally saved my life twice during her lifetime. It was mutual for me. I saved her life when I rescued her. Unfortunately, she passed away on June 23, 2013. God rest your soul, Miss Molly Sue. Get plenty of belly rubs and I will see you again someday.

My fur babies are very special to me. Dogs love so unconditionally. It is beyond me to understand how people can abuse animals. Although the meat isn't bad, I don't even like the thought of killing Bambi during deer season. Tennessee, by the way, passed a very important law called the Road Kill Law. If ya kill it with the car, it is okay to haul that animal away and not feel guilty that you were eating Bambi that Saturday night. Sounds a lot Southern and a bit redneck, but hey, Tennessee folks are always accused of being redneck hillbillies, so we might as well act like it I guess. It's not just Tennessee.

The state of Georgia is equally Southern. In fact, rednecks exist in ALL states, including those Northern Yankees. Having moved to South Florida nine months ago, I can tell you no one who lives in Florida are really from Florida. We are all legal immigrants in search of sunshine and salty air. Of course, no one told us about the NoSim mosquitos, neighborhood alligators that walk down the street like they own the place and birds the size of an adult dog. They too are not intimidated by humans or other animals.

Actually, where we live, we are the visitors that invade the animal's habitat. Tuff, the alligator can sun bathe beside the canal as long as he is across the canal in our neighbor's yard. The birds are beautiful but that too could peck your eyes out in a flash. Our little Yorki dog, Sissy, is fearless and Tuff, the Gator, would just as soon have her as an appetizer before his evening meal of Roast Duck. Someone told me to carry around a raw hunk of steak and if Tuff were to come to pay us a visit, I am to throw that steak as far as I could to distract him from my legs, arms and the family dogs. I'm no genius, but wouldn't that encourage Tuff to visit more often in search of his next grilled steak dinner? That could become quite costly to have another mouth to feed at dinner time. No, I think I will just stay my distance and encourage Tuff to work on his tan at the neighbor's back yard and we will mind our own business. Now I know why the Florida fans call their stadium the Swamp. It gets mighty swampy when you deal with nasty looking gators. When Tuff gets 6 feet, the animal control folks will come and have him relocated. But I feel sorry for Tuff and would probably not call the gator police on him. What are they trying to do? Are they making nice alligator purses each year? I don't want Tuff to have to deal with gator jail or the possibility of death row. It just ain't right, as we say in the South!

ARE ONLINE DATES ONLY WHERE FROGS GO FOR LOVE?

Okay, what happens in today's world of high technology and electronic social media? One advantage to on line dating is the ability to search for what you are really looking for in a mate. You can browse the many shapes and sizes of singles. It sounds perfect, right? There is only problem. Some people feel compelled to stretch the truth a bit. Then others feel obsessed to out and out lie. After all, that single handsome dude that is a Civil Engineer working overseas on a multimillion dollar project that fell in love with you at first look when he reviewed your picture. It's funny how one should be able to see right through that bull s**t, but when you get lonely and his profile exactly coincides with what your profile says you want, how could you go wrong? For that matter, if you try the bar fly approach, how do you know the life story is all that needs to be said? If you think about it, even church is filled with dysfunctional crazies that sit in the pews and try to find themselves.

Single people past the age of 30 really have an unfair advantage. You see people at work, but they are usually someone else ex or someone's husband that is "separated"; or you later find out you are cousins! If things don't work out, you become the subject of today's gossip and labeled that middle aged single slut who is out to flirt, tease, and get their claws in any man that wants it. None of the traditional options for dating seemed to work and if you are in your 50s or 60s, you don't even have the workplace as a potential spot for perfect partners.

So, it's time to go online. First, decide what you want. Then, decide what you don't want. Then find a photo that is not too cleavage centered (especially if you have no real cleavage to show). Don't use your professional resume photo and don't look too motherly like. It's a turn off for some guys to see your profile picture of your dog or grandkid or politically preferred Presidential candidate. If you can't seem to find that photo, try making selfies for a week and see if you can't get that perfect look. Then go back to the cutest dog picture with a head shot of yourself at the beach with Fido with a nice glass of wine in your hand.

Beware of adding too many photos and delete the 'dancing on the bar' times with your girlfriends. They may like your other cute girlfriend better than you and that just ain't right. No sharing. It's every lady for herself when it comes to being on the hunt for that perfect Prince Charming. After all, you will soon find out that no matter how accurate your profile is and how cute that guy picture is, you WILL kiss a lot of frogs before Prince Charming shows up. Also, beware of thinking that you really finally found the Prince. We all are on our best behavior at first. It's the ugly side of each of us that surfaces much later.

Cinderella may look great at first, but beware that at the stroke of midnight that 10 may wake up as a 2. (Hear Kenny Chesney's song on the perfect 10 and why one might consider NOT doing the "nasty" until down the road when the ugly side starts to surface. Ask me sometime about what Woody Allen says about hitting the sack too soon with Mr. GQ. You might want to consider carrying a bag with you always in case the merchandise doesn't look as good as you thought when you drank that third shot of tequila last night.

By the way, I never said these were experiences I had and besides I would never tell anyway, unless you have a need to know. If you can't count your love slaves on two hands or you can't make a complete list because you quit counting, you may want to go back to the church boys that either go slow or don't talk about the ones that got away. Oh, Lord, I am so glad I'm off the market. My love life is starting to come back to mind and I can't tell you how many loser frogs I met. But there are a few frogs' worthy of mentioning.

Let's talk about Snaky Sam. There once was a boy named Snaky Sam (that's what I will call him to protect the innocent), who couldn't seem to decide what to do in life. He thought dress up meant wearing his favorite holey T-shirt and flip flops. He thought a first date included an escort for his young boy on the weekend all around to various Burger King's in his town for the usual fine dining. The youngster, among other play toys, had a pet snake in an aquarium in his room. His pet's name was Snaky. Snaky dined on frozen mice. Yep, you got it; straight from the freezer that the human beings also had their frozen produce stored. This place was the model man cave home. That's okay. I suspected as much on our first meet up when his attire was a hint of first impressions.

As I recall, the gentlemen stated he was 5'9", but I think I towered over him by at least 4" even with my smaller heels on. Shrinkage, as we grow older is a possibility, I guess. Besides, I never confirmed his height and why is that so important if you finally found your Prince Charming? Unless, of course, you wanted to go partying and the bartender carded him at age 53! I had him covered, however; they never card me anymore! Sorry, I digressed. I just had to get that one off my chest. (Not literally off my chest.) I visited his humble abode once and he wanted me to meet his son and his family and sleep in his son's room where Snaky rested. Sorry but that is just a bit too much to ask an ole girl to find true and lasting love.

After all, true love can't have limitations. Sleeping with a snake was a show stopper for me. By the way, this new boyfriend of mine was yet another unusual mode of heartache called, 'let's just quite communicating all together!' No more boyfriend, girlfriend that he said we were. No more being "in like" with each other. I guess true love, (the soul mate kind), still always has boundaries and conditions that just ain't gonna be overcome, no matter how big and how cute that damn snake was to get over the years!

By the way, after traveling all day and slumbering for a couple of hours to relax, I hear that kid scream from the kitchen that immediately woke me when he had taken snakey's mouse out and cut up his body parts to play with. He told his dad he was lying. Oops—that's when we realized his ADHD meds had been forgotten that day. Yep, just another day in paradise in the town of no return. Learnings:

Never enter into a relationship when the kid will always be number one, which by the way is what, ought to be in those formative years. But I refuse, at my age, to always be number 3, behind Snaky. My first meeting of a potential new friend presents the question like this: "You got any pets? What kind and exactly how close are they to you?" It's just like Molly Sue, my beloved Basset hound dog when it comes to companions. I would take a bullet for Molly; but never could visualize the same for Snaky.

If I had a gun that night and didn't think I would harm myself or others, Snaky would be at the dinner table the next evening. Another new rule was established at this point in the dating game. Never do a road show for any new friend/man/anybody. The exception might be a second or third meet up or if they own a beautiful oceanfront Villa on some tropical island. Rules can be made to be broken.

AM I REALLY CRAZY OR JUST ACT THAT WAY?

When do you transition from normal to semi-normal too crazy to bat-shit crazy? First of all, I don't believe there is a normal person alive today. It just depends on the relativeness of "crazy" and when you have your first meltdown. I have an old saying that I made up which goes like this…someone is having a conversation with you. We will assume that they are "normal." They say to you, "what? Are you crazy?" My rebuttal is that statement is YES! I am certified. It's you people in denial that I worry about! The crazy people who are borderline bat shit crazy laugh uncontrollably. They get it.

The folks that are on the edge of their first melt down felt a flush over them, followed by severe panic and worry. But the folks that don't get it, are the very ones to watch out for. I must say that I am not in favor of pushing another pill your way. One if you are sad; another is if you are too glad or manic; and one is if you can't sleep; and a final one is if you sleep too much. When does that pill cocktail stop? I am not a fan of those bi-polar victims that think they are healed when they wake up in that euphoric manic stage.

Many of those with bi-polar disorder can never predict when they will have an up day and when it's time to drag yourself back to bed with the covers over your head in their bad day phase. As an individual who suffers from Chronic clinical depression let me state my pet peeve. When referring to a friend or family member, please do not say, "They are crazy. They are bi-polar" No, ladies and gentlemen, that are not bi-polar; they have bi-polar disorder and when treated with appropriate diet, exercise, and medication, they are great fun to be around.

But you may feel like they have multi-personality disorder when the roller coaster of living with this disease becomes too much to handle. Folks don't know how to act when an individual is plagued with PTSD. I met a veteran who was so jumpy; he lived in constant paranoia thinking the living hell of war was still there.

Those OCD friends that are beyond being obsessively neat and orderly will have to watch where they walk to avoid stepping on a crack that will break your mother's back. I know someone that has to flick the lights on and off 13 times before leaving a room. Thirteen is significant for him and the process is critical before leaving his home. You just thought he was checking the house for locked doors. Many young mothers are labeled OCD because we must learn to manage the home; the job, the kids, and the husband, in addition to making sure you have some resemblance of project managing your own life. That's about mastering the fine art of multi-tasking that many of my analytical male friends just can't manage.

I am not being politically incorrect nor discriminating against all men. I am merely stating a fact that as a young mother, you better go to multi-tasking school or you will die trying. Clinical depression is not about feeling down or having a bad hair day. Please don't tell me one more time to JUST GET OVER IT. Clinically depressed people are not lazy. They cannot help the way they feel. If you can catch the down feeling before you fall in the dark hole without a rope, you may be able to process some simple steps and overcome that chronically depressed state.

If the doctors have you on an anti-depressant for the right reasons, do not think that life is now beautiful and go off the meds cold turkey. It just will not work. However, I am always setting a goal to continue to reevaluate the proper level of medication that is required to avoid depression as I know it. When did I first notice depression that was impossible to overcome without help? I'm thinking it really started when I gave birth to my son in 1983. I didn't know it at the time, but sleep deprivation and constant change physically, emotionally, and mentally are the very triggers just before you reach that level of melt down.

If you are particularly Chatty by nature, an off the chain extravert and an eternal optimist (that believes the world is your oyster), when you get lonely, quiet, and introspective, folks think you must be sick. My mom, over the years, would force me to go to bed when I got beyond hyperactive transitioning to just plain weird. I have learned to avoid sleep deprivation at all costs. I must have 7-8 hours of sleep consistently to behave at that level of "normalcy." If I am talking in half sentences because I can't express myself fast enough, it's time to slow that train wreck down and take a power nap or lights out to sleep at night. I am, by nature, the morning person that gets up with the roosters.

I love the mornings and my hubby is just the opposite. The night owl gets his quiet time after midnight and my quiet time is between 6:00am and 9:00am. Once you get in a rhythm instead of trying to change your partner or try to change yourself, that quiet time becomes sacred. I learned and so did he. It's okay; after all, we are retired and that's what retired people do. (Any damn thing they want to do, including nothing).

Five o'clock somewhere becomes your island time zone and life is good. In fact, it's really good. You actually forgot what it was like to go to a job and work. It makes you wonder how you did everything you enjoy, raise kids, and climb the corporate ladder at the same time. Once those kids are off your payroll and out of the nest and your job replacement actually can carry on, you are free to enjoy life the way you always dreamed it could be. It leaves you with "living the dream" as your job description.

Retired is not unemployment or necessarily disabled. Retired is what we long for to acquire the status of "calling your own shots." Just make sure you aren't still in pajamas at happy hour time because people might label you crazy and senile and we know how hurtful those terms can be. If this does happen, make a run to Walmart and folks will understand. I long to be normal and once I figure out what that looks like and feels like, I will know that insanity is not a state of existence.

DO YOU HAVE TO GO OUT OF TOWN TO FIND YOUR SOULMATE?

When online dating has left you with no more available single candidates, I guess the answer is to widen your territory for possible winners. Maybe just 100 miles would open up all kinds of possibilities. All you have to do is go into your profile and change the search criteria and you will open a wild variety of both losers and winners. Is 100 miles far enough? Apparently, I had to travel at least 3 hours to find my prince.

Mom always said those online guys are nothing but scams and perverts and I should find a stable single gentleman another way. If you are in late 50s, which rock will you turn over to find the pot of gold at the end of the rainbow? So, I widened my search to at least cover 175 miles, plus or minus 25 more miles.

Yes, 200 miles is as far as I will go to even entertain the long distance relationship category. It took a while to set my limits but one night about 2 in the morning, I saw this drop dead handsome island boy type hidden in the hills of Georgia. Have you ever heard of Powder Springs, GA? I learned to MapQuest the distance and approximate location of Powder

Springs, GA. Okay, I will give it a try. It was worth it to find a Parrot head that is a good looking guy with a sweet and funny disposition. Mom always told me when I quit looking; he will be there right in front of you.

If that were true, why didn't I meet my hubby back on campus when we were in College? He majored in Geology and Environmental Engineering and LIFE; I majored in Business and Psychology and LIFE. His was a college cheerleader and frat boy and I was a majorette and sorority girl and little sister to another fraternity. Our college campus wasn't that big. We knew each other's friends and he even said he remembered me, but karma didn't kick in until 39 years later, when I quit looking. Mom was right, as usual.

But little did she know that I found him on the "Plenty of Fish" online dating site at 2 o'clock in the morning and 3 hours away. It beats finding him at some tiki bar being a bar fly while he flirted with me with intentions that might be less than appropriate. We talked for a month and a half and as the new rules set were, we decided to meet at the Homecoming game at our alma mater in October 2013.

That was half way and actually a little closer to

West Knoxville than he was to Chattanooga. Little did I know that he would be accompanied by his elderly Uncle and faithful dog, Tully. When he finally arrived at McDonalds, Uncle Peek was in the copilot seat and Tully and I were in the back seat side by side. Tully didn't care for me at first. In fact, in our first months of dating, he worked real hard to send me packing home to Tennessee. Tully is a cattle dog and his dad was his one and only owner.

He could not see a future in my intrusion into the family. Tully is very protective to his owner and will herd you and nip you if needed to reinforce that he is the Alpha dog. My Basset, Molly, didn't care for Tully and before Molly went to heaven (rip, dear girl); Molly bit Tully on the ear which left a permanent reminder to him of who the Alpha dog really was. Don't feel too sorry for Tully. He tore two pair of my favorite pants and only bit me four times before I threatened to call the dog police and send him off to dog jail for the third time.

When Tully finally realized that I was a keeper, we have become the best of buddies. I am his mom now and he would nip any and all Fed Ex men in uniform before they came close to his mom. I have to watch him to make sure he doesn't in up causing a law suit and off to dog jail he would go. Tully has since mellowed in his old age and now my little Yorkie mix rescue, Sissy, is the fearless wonder that would scare any and all strangers that came close to her mom and dad. I have to watch Sissy when we go outside.

She wants to play with all turtles, birds, and our occasional neighborhood alligator, Tuff. Tuff would just as soon have Sissy as his appetizer before taking on a bird and large turtle for dinner. Tuff minds his own business and I am constantly looking over my shoulder for a Tuff siting. To date, I have not had the pleasure of meeting Tuff face to face and that is just fine with me. I do have pictures of the old boy when he sunbathes across the canal from our house. Have a nice life, Tuff. When he becomes more than 5 feet, they will come relocate him to another home.

SHOULD WE GET MARRIED NOW THAT WE FINALLY MET?

Married? Is third time a charm? My future hubby was 0 for 2 and so was I. Is the old saying," Third time's a charm" where we are in life? I just picked one at number two and so did he. Did we just settle when our number 2 came along? What makes us think we are not settling again? After a year of traveling back and forth in our long distance relationship, we decided that number 3 was our best and final and we wanted to grow old with each other. Let's get those rings and marry before someone talks us out of it. Where would two Parrot head trop rock lovers get married to seal the deal forever? At the 2014 Meeting of the Minds festival in Key West, Florida. We went to Key West in my little Miata convertible for 10 days to make my virgin voyage to the island the most memorable vacation ever.

It was wonderful, adventuresome, without any witness or preacher until we got there. It also meant I had to travel the 7-mile bridge and I have a phobia for bridges. I figured if I could survive the 7-mile bridge without having a panic attack, it must be fate that we fell in love with each other. We stopped just before the bridge and had lunch and a few glasses of wine or three and I never knew we were even on the 7-mile journey until we were almost over the bridge. That wasn't nearly as bad as the Golden Gate Bridge or the one lane swinging bridge in Kingston, TN that I will never forget. I don't think either of those bridges really were swinging bridging, but it sure felt like it and that was a sure fire trigger for anxiety onset.

So, it's October 31 in Key West and we finally checked in to our first motel on Duvall Street. Hubby had been to Key West so many times that I think some of the street folks actually recognized him. He has Key West stories that I could never top. Let's just say that OUR trip to Key West was a one of a kind with our own sweet memories; and all other memories for him were his to remember and in the past.

When you are in your 50s, vacations are not your first rodeo with another person. My family vacations to Destin, FL will always have nice memories but those are in the past and it was now time to create our own memories with each other. Some folks get jealous of their new soul mates past relationships. I really want to go on record now to say I am not insecure nor jealous of other women from the past. I will however, say that sometimes it is best that one should stay in the past and not be a part of the present so much. It's not about low self-esteem or jealous or insecurity. It is about time.

Life is so short and it is time to create your own happiness. Hubby and I hope to celebrate at least 25 years together, but let's face it, the clock ticks on and we aren't getting any younger. In fact, it wasn't until this year when we both we in our 60s that we discovered we were old and were a part of the baby boomer's old fart club. We get senior discounts and we can now act a fool in public and people just write it off as two old seniors who don't realize that the new age doesn't dance like us. Personally, I love to dance and will be dancing on a cloud at my own funeral/celebration of life at age of 100-110, Lord willing.

WHERE DO YOU GO TO FIND PARADISE?

Hubby and I were undecided on next step but we were sure moving south was the right location. We thought about Chattanooga which would put us close to both of our mom's. It was also the town that brought us together. But that still had us facing winter months, although mild compared to our northern friend's homes. The process starts with Zillow. Zillow is a data base filled with all kinds of homes for sale anywhere you want to be. That was the first question. visit shortly after our Key West trip. It just didn't feel right.

We had friends in Venice, Florida and we took the scenic route from Key West to Venice, Florida. Venice was north of Cape Coral and south of Tampa. We decided on the west coast and set out to check out Venice and the surrounding areas. Venice is truly beautiful, but we couldn't find any real estate that was within our budget and didn't require doing a fixer upper project. We wanted to move in and enjoy in our own little piece of paradise.

After coming back to Georgia, we got the house on the market and continued our search for our dream home. In September 2015, we paid another visit to our friend's home in Venice and added a couple of days in a little town called Englewood. I found a condo on Beach Road in Englewood and we hooked up with the best realtor in this area. Our realtor found a half a dozen homes in addition to a few I found in the area from Zillow. After meeting him, we saw five homes that were within our budget and in the desired area. The first home we saw was a beautiful home with just about everything we desired, excluding a few minor negatives.

The next to the last home was in a community called Rotonda West, Florida and we knew after the first time we walked in the front door that it was our home forever. Our home is in a community of approximately 8,000 people with the average age during off season of 65 and during the snow bird season, the average jumps to close to 70.

Yep, we are the youngsters of the neighborhood. It is a community with history from the native Indians. The Indians knew what they were doing when they settled on this land. It feels like we are in the witness-protection program. No one has ever heard of Rotonda West. If you google the area and zoom in, we live in a wagon wheel which is often described as the circle. If you look at the map, we are about 10 o'clock on the face of a clock as you look at the circle.

We are about 10 minutes to the beach at Manasota Key and nestled between Venice and Port Charlotte, Florida. This is our little piece of paradise. When it's hotter than hell, we go out the back door and jump in our pool. If you want to gaze at more water, we have canals on two sides of us. Of course, we are about 20 minutes to our friends in Venice. The disadvantage is we are 700 miles from my hometown of Knoxville, TN where my mom and sister still reside. Mom lives in a senior community that is quite upscale.

This Senior living community is a chapter all to itself. It is like a very large cruise ship on land. Mom loves it and I am so happy she is taken care of since 700 miles is the longest distance away from her ever. I have plenty of friends still in my hometown, including our church family and my sister. My brother lives in Statesville, NC. My son and his family live in Nashville, TN. When we go north to visit, we travel to Atlanta area, Chattanooga, Nashville, and Knoxville. It is quite a trip, but it's our way on keeping the friends and family that love us and we love as well.

Quite a few of our Georgia and Tennessee friends have visited and that brings us close to our roots and prevents that homesick feeling when you realize we are starting over to rebuild our friends and extended family. The year 2015/2016 has been two years of constant change. Unfortunately, they were not all positives. After our first visit home, my hubby's mom's health took a turn for the worse and just as we got the dogs from the kennel and finished up the laundry from a whirlwind 10-day trip, we got the call that Ms. Betty had passed away. We had to board the dogs again and head back out to coordinate a funeral, ology, graveside and handling the final arrangements for closing out his mom's affairs.

That trip was exhausting, full of grief, and although we got to see a lot of our old friends and family, it left us with emptiness beyond any grief we had experienced. The exception was the year before; we had to bury Uncle Peek which was like a second father to my hubby and his family. Peek never married, had no children and lived with his family all his life.

He also lived with hubby in the Powder Springs home the final two years of his life before the dreaded Alzheimer's disease took over. Two deaths the first two years of our lives together was tough for both of us. I am glad that I was with hubby to offer support during the most difficult time of his life.

We moved the end of December 2015 and Betty passed away in February 2016. My mom had her share of health scares as well and in July 2016, she suffered a TIA (mini stroke), which left her with temporary memory loss and a lot of stress and anxiety that she might never gain her full functioning mind back. Her father had died of Alzheimer's and our biggest worry was the onset of dementia or Alzheimer's since the gene was so close to home. The good news is she has regained a lot of her memory back and continues to live in the senior living community she calls paradise.

HOW DOES ONE TRAIN FOR SENIOR STATUS THAT MOST CALL ELDERLY OLD FARTS?

How does one prepare for the reality of getting old? You know you are old when you either have to have a power nap during the day or hit the sack by 10:00pm. Retirement doesn't help any when you wake up each morning and every day feels like the weekend. On the one hand, that is everyone's dream. But on the other hand, running to the calendar each day and checking your cell phone for the date and what you have to accomplish is really a pain.

The good news is if you forget the honey do list or it gets past 3:00pm, you get used to justifying procrastinating by using the phase, "let's do that tomorrow, when we aren't so busy." I mean the world will not stop if we choose an early happy hour and opt to play in the pool and harass the doggies all day. We have made a lot of improvements to our little house in the witness-protection program. July 26, 2016 was hubby's Birthday and we invited close friends and neighbors to join us poolside for our version of a trop rock party, complete with live music by our dear friend from Atlanta, GA. Several Georgia and Tennessee friends joined us for several days and it was perfect for ringing in senior status for hubby.

The sixties aren't as bad as I imaged really, especially since we are in the youngster age bracket compared to the Englewood/Rotonda community. What more could I ask for from the last two years of life. I have managed to dodge Cancer, find and marry Prince Charming, welcome the most adorable little granddaughter into this world. She turns two years old this month and has a little sister on the way in December.

I have a beautiful home with two wonderful doggies and even a resident neighborhood alligator we call Tuff. The neighbors said Tuff was 15 feet but after he grows to 5 feet or more, they relocate the boy to another unknown location. We think after seeing Tuff for the first time at the birthday party, he looked more like about 4 feet.

Regardless, as long as he does his sunbathing across the canal in the neighbor's yard, I am okay with him living in our community. After all, he had seniority on us and by rights we should be the first to have to relocate. Another wonderful thing about the area we live in is the talent of musicians that live around our town.

On any given evening, we can catch a live show with some very good musicians that have played for years with Jimmy Buffett and the Coral Reefers Band. Unfortunately, we lost another dear friend and very talented musician this summer. Jim Morris had long been a favorite of ours with just the right style of music and song writing. Jim passed away suddenly at age 64 with a double aneurism and after passing out in front of his band members at the airport, he never regained consciousness.

A favorite song that Jim wrote became his mode of leaving this earth as we know it. Jim's song is titled, "Living til the day I die." He truly lived a full life and left a legacy of music for all of us to enjoy forever. Jim had at least 2,000 fans at his Celebration of Life event which brought many great musicians that not only respected Jim for his music but loved him as we all did for who Jim was as a man and friend.

HOW DO YOU ELIMINATE LIFE'S HEARTACHES AND LIVE HAPPINESS UNTIL THE DAY WE DIE?

It has taken me 61 years of living and nearly dying to realize the reality of God's gift of life he has given us. No matter how hard I try, God never promised us a life of pure bliss. I live each day hoping to experience far more moments of joy versus heartaches of suffering over loneliness, fear, depression, stress, disease, and deep seeded suffering by grieving those that have gone before us. Life is truly worth living and I never have contemplated terminating my life because of the heartaches and suffering. Life is not about the breathes we take, but about the moments that take our breathe away. I truly believe I have applied that knowledge I have gained through research, book learning, education, and the school of hard knocks. I have gained that wisdom by making mistakes along the way, listening and learning from my elders that love and care about me, and the desire to continue to grow through adventures that I have never experienced. I call that "calculated risk taking and doing everything in moderation, most of the time." When I have abused the moderation rule, I sure learned my lessons by accepting the consequences for making a bad decision. Just like my mama and daddy always said, "Never accept no for an answer when you know in your heart it is something that is the right choice to make in order to fulfill everlasting happiness.

DID I TELL YOU ALL MY SECRETS?

Now I am no fool. After all, I have a reputation to maintain and I hopefully haven't embarrassed and disappointed my family and especially my son. My son is my legacy and I could not be more proud of the man he has become. We both worked hard to grow up together. I tried to instill values and work ethics that mean something. I tried to show him what good outcomes come from working hard. I tried to allow him to see me cry when I hurt and I hope he realizes that obstacles can be overcome if you have the faith that the Good Lord has shared so that we may live a fulfilled life in our Christian walk.

It makes the subject of death something not to be feared; and when our time is up, we can travel spiritually to eternity where we will meet up with our loved ones in heaven. I know for a fact, there will be a group of sweet dogs that will be led by Molly Sue waiting for belly rubs and lots of kisses. Our disabilities will be no more and we will be free of jealousy, hate, fear, terror, evil and those that participated in your heartache experiences will be forgiven and forgotten. Life will be as we dream, free of the bad stuff and complete with all the good stuff we could ever imagine. I hope to surround myself in heaven with my family, heroes, mentors, friends that offer unconditional love and the entire animal I ever wanted to love and nurture. I have realized my piece of paradise with the man of my dreams. Let's play out this journey until death do us part.

A NEW DIAGNOSIS — GEOGRAPHICALLY CHALLENGED

Some of us are plagued with this dreaded illness of not being able to find my way to the mailbox without getting lost. I told my husband there is always another scenic route to take to get from point A to point B. Like the time I got lost in Chattanooga on the way to Georgia. It was my visit to Powder Springs, GA and I thought he was going to have to come after me. In fact, leaving to go back home was another disaster. I took one wrong turn and suddenly I was on the other side of Atlanta in unfamiliar territory. I called Bobby again and he literally had me stop at a post office on a Sunday afternoon and he escorted me to the interstate. I think he took pride in ribbing me about my disability and I failed to see the humor.

To make fun of someone for a disability just is not politically correct. I have made it a point to go a different way to the grocery store in our new home and frankly, I know my way around a lot better than you know who. Of course, he would not admit it. When we moved to Florida, it was 2am in the morning with two cars and two dogs coming into Rotonda West.

We came a very long way (thank you, Siri) to get

5 miles down the road to our neighborhood. I really did not want to call our realtor at that time and ask him for directions to what felt like an imaginary community. I told you we were convinced that we had bought a home in the witness protection program. People still think we made this place up and my mom is convinced that our address is just this side of falling into the Gulf of Mexico.

When it rains or storms in Rotonda West, we get frantic calls from family and friends to evacuate before the hurricane arrives. I swear we would be playing in the pool with the sun shining brightly when calls come in and prayer chains begin for our safety. Where I will take any prayers I can get, please save those for when the storms really arrive. It may be tomorrow but they haven't hit for 10 years. I guess we are due a big tropical storm. We are right around the corner from the middle school where we vote and more importantly, where we evacuate to. Rehearsing for the big storm becomes a community requirement.

Having grown up in the weapons plant community, we had walk outs from school to home in case of a nuclear attack. We would file out of the school without talking and in single file to walk home and head for our basement fallout shelter. It took me into adulthood before I realized other kids never worried about such things. Our fallout shelter was full of water and nonperishables. As I think about it, being in a space the size of a small closet with all five of us in the family clan would have been very uncomfortable. I'm not sure if it wouldn't be better to just risk the nuclear explosion versus living in a hole with my siblings and two adults. I am sure dad hid a bottle of Vodka in the shelter to minimize his anxiety.

    Knowing dad, we would have been proofreading his Maintenance procedures that were in draft for dad's work. My family worked hard and played hard. I cannot complain about my younger years; in spite of the medical issues I overcame. If we weren't eating hot dogs at the baseball field, we were at the high school football field or taking swimming lessons at the local golf and country club.

    We belonged to local Golf and Country Club but we never played golf. It was the social membership that my parents had to ensure we had opportunities to meet and greet other families in our community. It never occurred any of us to buy some golf clubs and learn how to play. You should see me swing a golf club.

    Playing nine holes with me is like waiting through

a four hour Gone with the Wind showing. I had difficulty hitting the ball without digging up the grass and I probably would have gotten lost searching for the ninth hole, due to my geographically challenged disability. Oh well, that's what GPS and the Siri lady are for. I threw away the GPS when they had me going to Georgia via Nashville instead of I75. I tried to explain to hubby that getting lost was not my fault. Siri gets me lost to try to pick a fight and I know some computer geek is laughing when she has been going to Chattanooga, by way of Omaha.

HOW CAN YOU PREDICT THE FUTURE WHEN YOU CAN'T FIND YOUR WAY?

I have given you just a sneak peak of the antics of my life in this publication. If you enjoyed taking the journey down memory lane with me, then perhaps you can help guide me into the future by way of adventures that I don't yet know or even dreamed of experiencing. I look so forward to growing old with my Prince. I pray twice daily at least that keeps me as centered and focused as possible. Many of the past heartaches still tug at my heart, such as deaths of best friends, loved ones, and puppy dog companions.

I know for a fact that dying is reality and I don't think you can ever prepare yourself for saying goodbye. The comforting thought that one day we will all reunite with a fresh spirit and new body with no more suffering. Molly will be standing at the pearly gates waiting for her belly rubs. Nanny and Granddaddy and dad and my best friend, Vicky, will wonder what kept me on earth so long. We just can't pick a date to expire. A wise Indian decided today was the day to die. He had experienced enough on the earth. He walked to an open field and built a make shift bed that would serve as his final resting place. He jumps up on the bed and crosses his chest with his arms in preparation for his final breath. Closing his eyes, he starts to feel rain drops and before you know it, it is raining cats and dogs.

Immediately, he jumps up out of his trance and speaks to God on high. Okay, maybe today is not the day, Lord. I will come back when you need me. Whether my final breathe is tomorrow, age 100 or beyond, I am ready for my final resting place.

I will miss my loved ones on earth, but will be someone's guardian angel in heaven trying to drop pennies from heaven to signal those left on earth that I still am watching over you—'til death do you part. I have a lot of life left in me and plan to begin my journey into the second phase of life; but until then, let's live in the moment with all the joy in our heart we can. See you on the other side—someday.

LIVING HAPPILY EVER AFTER

One would almost always decide to end a memoir with a happy ending. Here goes. How could life get much better? I am retired, which means my days are filled with wants and a few needs; but always flexible to opt for nothing. We begin our Sundays with some meditation (my private time) to recenter my week. I miss the social interaction of church; but at so many levels, this social butterfly continues to be challenged to be silent with oneself.

As you know by now, I continue to search for who I really am. My CKisms continue: When do you gain so much knowledge that you forget to apply your learnings so it will transform to wisdom? I love to learn. My advanced studies concluded that there is no such thing as a finished education. Learning is a composition of book learning, classes, mentoring, trial and error, watching others, and going to places no one has ever been. I really don't favor research as my preferred learning style, although I am constantly using internet to satisfy my thirst for information. A quote on Facebook today reminded me of this.

You MUST believe the internet and Facebook—it's

as gospel as Jerry Springer, CNN and the National Enquirer. However, be careful when looking up medical symptoms. The internet will have you diagnosed with a terminal brain tumor when you have a headache. Before Monday, you will find yourself completing the final draft of your obituary, updating your will, putting your china on EBay and getting a down payment on a nice urn for the Funeral. (It's okay, son; I already have a nice urn inherited from my grandmother.

If you can't find it, the dog's ashes are in the other one that is proudly displayed on the bookshelf. Use it and mix my ashes with Molly Sue's ashes so we can live happily ever after) No worries on the subject of death.

This 3-time Cancer Survivor still has at least two lives left of the nine lives the Lord provided. I plan on living until 110, unless my quality of life is less than desired and then age 100 will be good enough. Speaking of good enough, that motto never really turned me on. Doing my best was a better approach. You see, life can be played like chess, making strategic moves until you win. Than if that is the best we can do, play life out more like poker; win after you look at the hand you are dealt, in the moment, and alter your approach as you go. In other words, know when to hold em and know when to fold em. Let's check off the bucket list now:

(1) Find the love of my life that you want to grow old with (October 19. 2013-check)

(2) Make a commitment on the beach at sunset in Key West (Nov 2, 2014-check)

(3) Pack up your life in Tennessee and search for our little piece of paradise in South Florida (December 28, 2015-check)

(4) Maintain a healthy lifestyle that will protect my kidneys, vital organs, diabetes, post Cancer, a balanced exercise rigor, good eating and drinking in moderation (August 21, 2016, ok, it's a work in progress – check)

(5) Enjoy the love of life daily with a large dose of living in the moment, adventure topped off with an overload of laughter, silliness and love for mankind and the animal kingdom.

(6) Begin working on a sequel to this publication in 2017 until the day I die (that gives me 39 more years – check)

(7) Balance my "me" time to enjoy my family, loved ones, and many good friends. (1991-present – check)

(8) Don't forget to say my prayers twice daily, as religiously as brushing my teeth. (2014-present and til death do us part – check mate!!)

What a blessing my life has been, I would to leave you with some words of wisdom:

   1. Do not fear the unknown.
   2. You can't die when you want to (SUICIDE AND OTHER MENTAL HEALTH MAY BE DIFFERENT ANSWER)
   3. Cherish you living loved ones while you can. After death, you still have those wonderful memories.
   4. Take charge of your own body with help from health care providers
   5. Lastly, NEVER ask God and others, WHY ME?

I invite you to my Sequel—NOT MY PEOPLE

AN INTRODUCTION TO THE ROLE OF THE SENIOR CAREGIVER AS WELL AS THE VICTIM OF DEVASTATING MENTAL DISORDERS, ESPECIALLY DEMENTIA AND ALZHEIMERS, SO PLLEASE JOIN US. I FORTUNATELY HAVE HANDS ON EXPERIENCE—TRYING TO CARE FOR MOM WITHOUT A ROADMAP.

SO, THE JOURNEY CONTINUES.......

Special Words: There Is one more lesson to learn that I give all the credit to my mom. She may not realize it, but patience is key to success. As a survivor, I have been blessed to handle my own challenges, but as a caregiver, it is much different. Read along in the second part of this book and you will see how hard the caregiver role can be.

AUTHOR'S GALLERY OVER THE YEARS

Figure 1. Having her first New Year's Eve celebration in Florida

Figure 2. SW Florida—My Paradise

Figure 3. Beautiful Scenery

Figure 4. Growing up together with my son

Figure 5. A NIGHT OUT MOM AND HUSBAND, BOBBY

Figure 6. Mom and I drinking our adult beverage

Figure 7. The house hunting trip when we found our Florida home

Figure 8. Beautiful in Paradise

Figure 9. Me and son just clowning around

Figure 10. Me and my son on his graduation day

Figure 11. My daughter-in-law and grandkids

Figure 12. My son and grandkid

Figure 13. My son and grandkid

Figure 14. My son's beautiful family

Figure 15. Sissy, our beloved rescue

Figure 16. Me and Bobby, my husband

Figure 17. My son and I celebrating my advanced degree.

Figure 18. Jason was born a Tennessee fan

Figure 19. My Adorable Grandkids

Figure 20. Bobby and our grandkid

Figure 21. Our adorable dog

Figure 22. Jason on the left with his two best friends from childhood

www.ingramcontent.com/pod-product-compliance
Lightning Source LLC
Chambersburg PA
CBHW050740080526
44579CB00017B/90